The
Good
Remembering

A Message for Our Times

by Llyn Roberts

BOOKS

Winchester, U.K.
New York, U.S.A.

First published by O Books, 2007
O Books is an imprint of John Hunt Publishing Ltd.,
The Bothy, Deershot Lodge, Park Lane, Ropley, Hants, SO24 0BE, UK
office1@o-books.net
www.o-books.net

Distribution in:

UK and Europe
Orca Book Services
orders@orcabookservices.co.uk
Tel: 01202 665432
Fax: 01202 666219 Int. code (44)

USA and Canada
NBN
custserv@nbnbooks.com
Tel: 1 800 462 6420
Fax: 1 800 338 4550

Australia and New Zealand
Brumby Books
sales@brumbybooks.com.au
Tel: 61 3 9761 5535
Fax: 61 3 9761 7095

Far East (offices in Singapore, Thailand,
Hong Kong, Taiwan)
Pansing Distribution Pte Ltd
kemal@pansing.com
Tel: 65 6319 9939
Fax: 65 6462 5761

South Africa
Alternative Books
altbook@peterhyde.co.za
Tel: 021 447 5300
Fax: 021 447 1430

Text copyright Llyn Roberts 2007
Design: Jim Weaver

ISBN-13: 978 1 84694 038 5
ISBN-10: 1 84694 038 9

A CIP catalogue record for this book is available from the
British Library.

Printed and bound by CPI Group (UK) Ltd, Croydon, CR0 4YY

Endorsements for *The Good Remembering* by Llyn Roberts

"I stumbled into ***The Good Remembering*** and felt compelled to read it from cover to cover. Now I recommend it to anyone searching for insight into spiritual growth during these intense times. Responsibly and well-written, it is a magical, powerful little book that transcends words and speaks directly to soul."

> – **Melody Beattie,** New York Times Best Selling Author of *Co-Dependent No More* and of *Finding Your Way Home, A Soul Survival Kit* (with excerpts from *The Good Remembering*), and many other books.

"***The Good Remembering*** offers valuable insight and guidance for relating to these times of accelerated personal and global change. Everyone should read this book! Anyone interested in more fully participating in life will value it immensely."

> – **Donald M. Epstein, D.C.**, Developer of Network Chiropractic/Network Spinal Analysis and author of books including *The Twelve Stages of Healing* and *Healing Myths, Healing Magic*.

"Llyn Roberts shares in a brilliant way a new vision for the future. ***The Good Remembering*** provides inspiration that we all need right now."

> – **Sandra Ingerman**, author of *Soul Retrieval* and *Medicine for the Earth*.

"(***The Good Remembering***)...brings together so many things that need to be together."

> – **John E. Mack, M.D.** Harvard professor and Pulitzer Prize-winning author of *A Prince of Our Disorder: The Life of T.E. Lawrence*, and *Passport to the Cosmos*.

Author's Acknowledgements

For believing what appeared beyond belief, I thank Crystena Daves-Brody. For support, encouragement and clarity, I thank Brian Luke Seaward. For urging me to publish *The Good Remembering*, I am grateful to Melody Beattie. I thank Dr. Joel Shrut for his timely love and guidance, and Beth Power for being a true and skillful friend. I thank Dr. Donald M. Epstein, as well as Kathlyn and Gay Hendricks, for their transformational and integrative work. For editing and printing the original material I thank Gail Holmgren-Bickford of Freedom Press Associates. For his support of this book I thank Michael Herrick. I am grateful to my family and my Catholic heritage.

My gratitude goes to dear friends, apprentices and students, spiritual teachers and respected colleagues prior to and within my work at Dream Change, and to project partners Bob Southard, Robert Levy and Bill Pfeiffer. I thank my publisher, John Hunt, for his vision, integrity and direction; the late Dr. John Mack, Bernardo and Cleicha Peixoto, Peter Clark, Ray Demers, Charles Farrell, Laurie Farrell, Sue Jamieson, Joel Kaplan, Kari Lygren, Nancy Postier, El Williamson, Wendy

Taylor and the many who supported this book's passage. I thank Patti Roberts Chiburis for being there throughout.

I am grateful to my Tibetan, Quechua, Amazonian, Siberian, Maya and other elders, teachers, sisters and brothers – and the lands and spirits that infuse them. I thank all compassionate beings and wakeful energies. For rejoining me with the star people of my childhood I am indebted to my son Eben Michael Roberts Herrick. For sharing the journey with a wakeful soul I honor and thank my daughter Sayre Allyn Herrick. I thank John Perkins whose friendship, direction, encouragement, love, support, mentorship, vision, and persistence have made it possible for me to share this message.

For remembering us to the love and beauty of all that is and for the promise of a wakeful world: I thank our starry brothers and sisters, the Guardians of the Light – and you.

Foreword

These are exciting times to be alive! While it may seem that the world is heading into a state of chaos, a more accurate description would be evolution. Times of evolution, like the birth of a child, are exciting, if not exhilarating. And these are exciting times. Of course, not everyone who sees change coming embraces it. Being forced to move outside our comfort zones often causes tension and anxiety. But with exposure to any change, the distant becomes familiar, the unknown becomes known. Let there be no doubt. We as a human species, on the living planet we call earth, are undergoing change.

This change which is upon us is not a well-kept secret in the universe. Signs and prophecies have foretold the coming changes for millennia. Like the birth of a child, we can anticipate the arrival, yet we do not know the exact moment of birth. And so it is with the evolutionary process we find occurring here in our own back yard.

The Good Remembering tells us that the veils are disintegrating, like a cocoon that can no longer hold back the wings of flight. *The Good Remembering* invites us, encourages us to get off our feet and continue on the spiritual path toward home – to spread our wings and fly.

Through my journeys on the human path I have come across many books and sources of information claiming to help lift the veils of illusion and enlighten those who take their message to heart. Some channels and sources of transmission seem to convey their message with a touch of static or ego sifting. I have found Llyn's message to be a clear transmission, and although it is important for readers to discern for themselves the relevance of the message, you will find that every word was carefully chosen by the author for relevance, clarity and compassion.

So prepare to lift the veils of illusion as you turn these pages, and as you do, you will learn that you play an essential role in the unfolding of the universe.

Best wishes and inner peace,
Brian Luke Seaward, Ph.D.

Brian Luke Seaward is the author of *Stressed is Desserts Spelled Backwards*; *Quiet Mind, Fearless Heart*; the acclaimed *Stand Like Mountain, Flow Like Water: Reflections on Stress and Human Spirituality* and many other books. Seaward founded 'Inspirations Unlimited' and 'The Paramount Wellness Institute' in Boulder, Co.

Contents

Practices

Introduction

By John Perkins
New York Times bestselling author

Receiving guidance from Guardians of the Light is a time-honored tradition. These powerful and often very timely messages have served spiritual leaders, shamans, artists, writers, and musicians since before recorded history. They are depicted on the earliest cave drawings and have been passed down through the ages by indigenous story-tellers.

The very word *inspiration* literally denotes being "in spirit". Homer invoked the aid of Greek Muses before writing his epics, the *Iliad* and the *Odyssey*. Moses, Christ, Muhammad, Buddha and religious leaders throughout the ages shared the teachings of their spiritual guardians with their followers. The list of those who have put such messages to more recent public use is long, including: the scientists Einstein, Burbank, Marconi, and Edison; the musicians Bach, Beethoven, Schumann, and Mozart; the writers Keats, Shelly, and Joyce; and the political leaders Roosevelt, Gandhi, and

Kennedy. There is a well-documented account about Winston Churchill during a 1941 air raid in London when the voice of a Guardian of the Light directed him away from a spot where a German bomb exploded seconds later.

Most indigenous cultures encourage their children to start heeding these messages at an early age. Throughout the Amazon, Andes, deserts of the Middle East, Siberian Steppes, the jungles of Asia, plains of Africa, and islands of Oceana tribal elders point to the heavens and tell younger generations to listen to the wisdom of their starry brothers and sisters. Children who are particularly adept at conveying the knowledge they receive are singled out as community leaders.

I can personally attest to the power of such messages. Raised as a Christian in Calvinistic New England, I talked with God, Jesus, and other Christian Guardians long before I learned to read and write. When I listened to their advice, I found I was well served; when I ignored it, I wished I had done otherwise. Traveling around the world as an economic hit man (EHM) in the 1970s, I surreptitiously sought out cultures that honored what they referred to as "spirit guides". I could not openly admit to these pursuits and keep my job, so I held my own council – and listened to theirs. I came to understand that there was a reason why I had been given a critical role in creating history's first truly global empire and that at some point I would arrive at a place where I could use my insider's information to work toward creating a better world for future generations.

My path took me to that place on 9/11. I was visiting the
Shuar of the Amazon that day and learned by two-way radio
about the tragic events in New York, Washington, and Penn-
sylvania. Shuar elders encouraged me to listen to the Guardians. Shortly after I returned to the States, I flew to Ground
Zero. Peering down into that smoldering pit, I listened. The
message came loud and clear that I should defer no longer.
Many people in my country were ignorant as to why we are
feared and hated by millions in other lands. I had to tell my
EHM story. I had to write *Confessions of an Economic Hit
Man*. I knew that I was being called to devote the rest of
my life to shapeshifting a culture that had lost touch with its
most fundamental ideals – those reflected in the Declaration
of Independence and our other sacred documents – into one
committed to creating a stable, sustainable, compassionate,
and peaceful world.

The messages Llyn Roberts shares with us in this remarkable book are profound – not because they are unique, but
because they are part of a time-honored tradition; because
they fill us with hope and inspire us to propel ourselves into
a future that our children will be grateful to inherit from us;
because they are messages intended for humanity in general,
not for her personally; because they were given to a woman
who was not a politician, writer, or religious leader, but was
rather a mother who had just experienced an extremely difficult, life-threatening child-birth; and because Llyn, like others before her who came from humble beginnings and were

given messages intended for humanity, possessed a deeply compassionate nature that compelled her to do whatever was necessary to share this profound message. A background that combined Catholicism, Buddhism, and indigenous shaman-ism, helped her understand that she had to overcome her shyness, an inherent reluctance to step into the public eye, in order to honor the messages she had received.

I have known Llyn since early 1997. Over the years we have taught workshops together and co-facilitated trips that take people to live with and learn from shamans deep in the Amazon rainforests and high in the Andes. Knowing her as well as I do and being a professional writer, I am especially fascinated to read the words in this book. If anyone ever was tempted to question their authenticity as channeled, I would respond that there is no way Llyn could have written these words by herself. She does not think, talk, or write like that.

In my own workshops, I began using many of the approaches described in the following pages a number of years ago – from an earlier manuscript Llyn had shared with me. Participants were deeply impacted by them. Many told me that their lives changed as a result – that they became more sensitive to the world around them, more present, more empowered to taking positive actions, and happier. I have always felt that the proof of such messages lies in their effectiveness. These certainly meet that test.

Llyn has been honored by wise elders in Siberia and Gua-temala, in addition to those in the Amazon and Andes, as a shaman and teacher. *The Good Remembering* is a tribute to those people, as well as to Llyn and the Guardians who entrusted her with their messages. She is stepping out into that public eye to share the message. It is imperative that we step out with her.

We have arrived at a crossroads in human history prophesized by many cultures as a time when people have an opportunity to rise to new levels of consciousness. These prophesies challenge us to evolve spiritually and emotionally. They emphasize that the conclusion is not inevitable; what happens next depends on how well we listen and how we act. The fate of children being born around the world rests with us – you and me – today. We must open our hearts, souls, and minds. We must listen to the messages in this amazing book. And we must take actions that will serve us, our children, grandchildren, and all sentient beings.

> **John Perkins** is the author of many books, a teacher, and founder of the non-profit Dream Change. His books have been printed in over 20 languages; *Confessions of an Economic Hit Man* was on many bestseller lists, including the *New York Times* for many months and where it was still listed at the time of this book's publication. Other books by him: *Shapeshifting, Spirit of the Shuar, The World Is As You Dream It, Psychonavigation,* and *The Stress-Free Habit.*

Author's Prologue

Beginning

In June of 1991 at age thirty three I gave birth at home to my second child, a ten pound two ounce boy. Delivering such a large baby almost killed us both. But by grace's hand my child survived and grew into a chubby, silk-skinned cherub. For me the birth initiated a life-changing spiritual awakening.

The spiritual world wasn't new to me. My maternal grandmother was raised by Catholic nuns in Canada and talked as a matter of course to saints, God and our dead relatives. Memere's allegiance to the spirit world made a lasting impression on me and I can still see her bony fingers rubbing prayers into the rosary that always draped her palm. The wooden beads now sit on my silk altar-top amidst sacred objects from all over the world.

One of the most remarkable stories of her family came after my grandmother's passing when her youngest daughter, my aunt Betty Lou, died of cancer. My Uncle Jake was awakened one night by a tune his mother sang to this child Betty, his sister, as a baby – "What'll I do when you have gone away?"

As Jake lay in bed an apparition emerged before him of the Virgin Mary and Betty Lou holding hands – both were veiled and dressed in ancient flowing garments. My aunt's eyes were closed yet she wore a smile of total contentment. Knowing the Blessed Mother was taking his sister to God, my uncle watched Mary let go of Betty's hands just as Jake's mother – my grandmother – entered the vision. Memere smiled at her son and took her daughter's hands into her own. The scene then faded and moments later the telephone rang. My uncle's beloved sister had died. Upon arriving at her house, Jake was startled to see on Betty Lou's face the smile of his vision. Her visitation greatly eased my uncle's loss.

However poignant my spiritual legacy, it is not unique. But "other-worldly" things are often suppressed or simply not shared. In just recent years my seventy-four year-old father told me that throughout his life he's consciously traveled in a spirit body, out of his physical body, to distant worlds while he's sleeping. My dad also claims an angel stands at the foot of his bed at night protecting him. My mother confirms this "angel" has even tugged on the blanket as they lay sleeping!

Throughout the decade of my twenties my inherited bent for the spiritual inspired me to live in India, study Tibetan Buddhism, practice yoga and become an energy healer. Yet nothing prepared me for what came next. In March of 1994, three years after my son Eben was born, my world seemed to change overnight. I feel that everything had led me to this moment.

Opening

The children were almost three and six and we lived outside Boulder, Colorado. My husband was between jobs, I was sick a lot and money was always tight. We had two beautiful children, yet these few years had been difficult, painful and lonely. And although my health had suffered since my son's birth my sensitivities had grown acute —currents of energy now moved through me as I had never experienced. I could see energies pulsing from the trees, earth and sky and as they pulsated within me I felt ecstatic, often sexual. Yet I could also be engulfed by grief from living so separately from nature and from the abuse of the earth I saw all around me. Emotions whipped through me like violent storms.

One night I collapsed onto the sofa in the living room after the children had gone to sleep. When our cat, Pearl, jumped onto my lap and began to knead her kitty claws into my thighs a thick sorrow seized my heart. My eyes brimmed with tears and my body began to shake, imperceptibly at first, yet soon it was heaving uncontrollably through my wrenching sobs. The release of emotion made my head feel odd, like my crown had opened up, naked to the universe. I knew that the veils between *this* and *other* worlds had evaporated. Then the hiss of an electric current shocked my ears and suddenly I was light as a feather. How could this be? I was lifting out of my body! I felt out of control, terrified that I was crazy. I couldn't breathe and it took concentrated effort to calm down.

Still shaken, the next day I sat down while the children were napping and I prayed. I asked God, the Buddhist lineage, spirit guides, whoever was out there to tell me what was happening to me and why. I resolved that whatever I wrote in the next few moments would give me the answers I needed. Even two sentences could reassure me.

Two sentences quickly became two pages and then several times a week for three months I was writing messages from *star beings*. I hid what I was doing from all but my closest friend. Without warning electric-like surges coursed through me and I scrambled for pen and notebook as the words flooded my mind. I knew this was *telepathy*, *channeling* or *automatic writing* and the words came almost too quickly to get them down. I was fully conscious and able to stop it if I wanted to, but I felt compelled to write and whenever I did, the energies in my body relaxed.

After three months the channeling suddenly stopped. But over the next two years my other-worldly experiences increased. Life for me and my family changed forever.

Other Realities and Energies

My perception was heightened in the years before and after the channeling which seemed to opened doorways to other worlds. I could, at times, hear distressed people calling from these other realities. Their voices assaulted my senses, anguished screams that yanked me from my world into theirs and turned my life inside-out.

At first terrified, I eventually learned to dissolve my fear; I'd know exactly what to do — I discovered that "passing souls" was second nature to me. Journeying consciously in *spirit* through a long circuitous tunnel, I felt every curve and movement as though having traveled this route a thousand times before. As I left this world for others, my physical body was frozen — lying, standing, sitting, or in whatever position I found myself when the voice called.

"Help me, help me!!!" The voice booms and I'm drawn out of my reality into another. My spirit speeds through a long tunnel to a vacant city lot where a gang delivers its final blows. His body goes down, head hitting hard on the cement. I rush to face him now and his eyes light as he sees me. "I love you Frank!" He dies. The force of my love propels his spirit out the top of his head and I fly him to the Light beings. This takes little time as measured in my world, even less in spirit world — a flash, a moment. Then I'm back through the tunnel, returning to my body.

I feel their despair and so many calling this time. From their dark outpost I feel the tugging but I'm afraid. I fight the pull and try to ignore them but I can't. My heart cracks open and I know I can help. I suddenly eject out — wince at the unease of leaving my body — then my spirit freed, fly through the tube to foreboding lands to retrieve lost souls. I see them, knowing my light is a beacon for those ripe to move on. I gather as many as I can, passing them instinctively through another long, dark tunnel and out the lighted end to luminous beings. Upon return I'm disoriented and exhausted. I can't focus for days.

My body seemed electrified during this time period. My daughter at seven had her own room but sometimes asked to sleep in "the big bed". One night I almost said no, knowing how sensitive I'd become. I invited Sayre in but asked her to give me lots of room. Several times that night I was jolted awake by strong electric-like shocks. Horrified, I could hardly sleep. Was I hallucinating? The next morning Sayre woke with a smile and said "Mommy, I kept moving away from you, making more room because every time I got next to you I got a big shock!"

It must have been this same energy that transformed my work. My body seemed a lightning rod attracting high voltage. In practicing Reiki, I felt thick currents streaming into me from the top of my head, penetrating to my root. Was this universal life force energy? A voice simply said "compassionate energies arise when they are needed". But this didn't express like Reiki hands-on healing. Instead, I started waving my hands wildly to pull in or cast out energies, whistling, making loud grunts and other sounds, forcefully blowing on my clients, clapping and snapping my fingers in the air around their bodies, and other such carryings-on. My clients benefited. To them it was obvious that I was no raving lunatic; they improved, healed, and recommended me to their friends. I wasn't *crazy*, but *ecstatic* – in a finely tuned state of awareness. As with Reiki, I opened like a hollow reed and the energy did through me what it was meant to do.

Intense and bizarre as these occurrences were, the most profound event of these times would prove the most challenging.

Initiation

For over nine days I was in continuous communication with spirits. I had trouble staying in *this* reality during this time – eating, sleeping, or even speaking to my children was often impossible. Thankfully, we lived isolated on a mountain and I managed the basics, struggling to stay in this world while at the same time navigating others.

It started during a lightning storm. I woke up in the middle of the night convinced I'd been struck by lightning. When I opened my eyes, a brilliant light flooded my room and four Light beings floated over me. I was stunned by the feelings that overwhelmed me – indescribable love and ravishing pleasure. Then I realized that I was experiencing *them*, I was merging with these Light beings! I cried, overwhelmed by bliss. My husband slept soundly through everything.

During the days and nights that followed the Light beings were constantly with me. Immersed in past and future lifetimes, they sometimes appeared in front of me as if on a movie screen. In and out of different realities, I was taught and healed by these spirits and initiated into the sacred energies of fire, water, and lightning. When walking on our mountain I saw Lights hovering over the tall grasses in the fields. The first time I saw them I asked "Are you nature energies or fairies, or what are you?" A voice responded "We are universal energies – what you perceive is the essence of your world. Everything is comprised of this Light."

One morning Christ appeared in my room. Enveloped in a glow that emanated love, his presence was palpable. His image then transformed into multitudes of Bodhisattvas extending as far as the eye could see – I knew these compassionate beings from the Buddhist tradition, those who had given up personal gain to benefit others. The Bodhisattvas radiated the same Light and love of Christ. Words cannot describe the power and beauty of these visions.

Despite the awe I experienced, after bouncing between worlds for nine days I was fragmented. I couldn't straddle realities anymore. My children were afraid because I couldn't listen to them long enough to be able to respond. The spirits told me it was time to go back to my own world, but I could not. Visions kept coming, seducing me into realities I now fought to ignore. I ate heavily – burgers, peanut butter and breads – anything to weigh me down, get me back in my body and slow the visions, keep me in *this* world. I prayed to the Buddhist lineage, to God. A lot of body/energy work and loving support from some tuned-in friends finally anchored me back. But it took weeks and months to fully integrate.

What was happening to me was sacred, even holy, but did it have to turn my world inside out?! I became frustrated in not fully understanding what I'd written, what to do about it, or how to stay grounded enough to figure it out. And never knowing what was coming next, profound and holy as it was, made me anxious, as did trying to be a good mother to two young children throughout whatever happened. Some of my friends thought I'd had a nervous breakdown. True, by now I was a different person. But taking this projection to heart wasn't going to benefit anyone and it did nothing to honor my experiences. For this, I looked to shamanism.

Indigenous Wisdom

Early in 1997 I met and started working with John Perkins who founded the non– profit organization, Dream Change. Since the 1960s, John had lived and studied with indigenous shamanic peoples in diverse parts of the world. Over the next years I facilitated trips with John for people wanting to learn from indigenous cultures; later I created my own trips. I traveled out of the country innumerable times – including to shamans and elders living in remote regions of the Amazon basin, the Asian steppes, the high Andes and in the ancient lands of Central America's Maya.

Immersing in shamanism was like turning the light switch on in a dark room. Visions and spirit contact were natural to indigenous shamanic peoples, in fact *vital* to their well being. Shamans related intimately with unseen energies – receiving *and heeding* – the messages of dreams and events, from plants and animals, spirit apparitions, even *starry visitors.* Native myths and folklore the world over told of peoples and ancestors from the stars. The name of a small tribe in Brazil, Ureu-eu Wau-Wau, literally means *people from the stars*; the Ogalala Sioux looked for divine messages from the star people sketched on stones; the Cherokee traced their origins to the Pleiades; the Shuar of the Amazon welcomed starry ancestors who appeared to them as balls of light in the night skies; Tuvans listened to the stars for signs and divination, and African lore tells of star people coming down from the heavens in 'magic sky boats' for thousands of years.

And not only was the "soul passing" that was so familiar to me by now a recognized shamanic practice, each tradition tapped the powers of the elements as spirit had inducted for me – most indigenous approaches even mirrored my "far-out" healing ways! Living with Tuvans in the taiga and on the Asian steppe, performing twelve thousand year old ceremony with Maya elders, initiating into water, fire, and plant spirits with the Quechua on revered volcanoes and with Amazonian peoples deep in the rainforest – was like coming home. I discovered that experiences like mine marked the medicine people of many cultures – there were even *lightning* shamans!

Though human as any of us and far from perfect, indigenous wisdom keepers were the healers of their communities and more – they were spiritual mediators balancing the relationship between people, earth and cosmos.

Years of intimate contact with indigenous peoples and the traditions, lands and spirits infusing them, gave me a profound sense of belonging. Not only had every piece of my experience finally found its fit, I was encouraged to embrace its power. As I did, *The Good Remembering* became clear.

Bringing it Home

Intense spiritual experiences continue for me; however, they now integrate quickly. I'm particularly prone to premonitions about the social and climate changes occurring throughout the planet now – and the opportunities that underlie them.

I've learned that my sensitivities aren't unique. In working with hundreds of people in recent years I've come to believe we're all innately capable of receiving messages from sources not identified by science. As indigenous shamanic cultures across the world teach, each of us can attune to the signs all around us to find our way through change. By aligning with deeper rhythms we can engage the living intelligence to which we're all connected. Not only is this important and ecstatic work, it may be a key to the survival of our own and many other species.

This period in human history begs us to go very deep. We must rouse our courage and inspire each other to step into new of ways of living and being. The days of the great outward and physical exploration of our planet may be over – those men and women who roamed unmapped mountains, deserts, oceans, and jungles – but the new vistas promise to be just as enticing; they are uniquely challenging and important.

It's been touching for me to watch the impact indigenous teachers have had on the people I've traveled with to the Amazon, Andes, Siberia, and Guatemalan highlands; they've returned to their work and families as changed people. I'm comfortable in generalizing that these women and men became more relaxed, authentic, and accepting of the "unexplainable" – experiences such as those you'll read about in the following pages. They came back with an expanded view of reality, helping them more perceptively relate to the pressing issues we all face today. Especially intriguing are the experiences of medical doctors, physicists, engineers, and others trained in the modern sciences:

"I understand now," a Ph.D. biologist said, "that I've always followed 'voices'. I called them 'inductive reasoning' or 'intuition', and used them to guide me in selecting samples to study, lists of data to analyze, things like that. I was always a bit embarrassed by them, tried to cover them up, explain them away. Now I know they're very human, part of my heritage and that I not only can accept, but also honor them. The more I thought about this, the more I came to realize that history's greatest scientific moments – those of Edison,

Einstein, and today's Quantum Physicists – often arrived through such 'voices'."

Some have wondered if being a woman and *not* having the demands they perceive are placed on men in my culture to inhibit emotions, such as sadness and fear, has made it easier for me to open to this journey. It's true that my emotions facilitated this passage, helping me to receive as well as share its gifts. They are also fundamental to the intuitive wisdom I still obtain – not necessarily "channeled" material, but guidance gleaned through sense, imagination, and longing. *The Good Remembering* invites this very process. If this is considered a "feminine way" I know it's intrinsic to all of us, men and women alike. Indigenous shamanic men, for example, are encouraged to open to their feelings and to experiences like the ones described in this book. Although some men in modern cultures have succeeded in integrating their yin and yang traits – we would do well to hearten *all* of our men to open to these aspects of themselves. And bring intuitive, sensual, earth and soul honoring qualities into our workplaces, schools and institutions. Only by creating conscious, embodied community will we and our children know a harmonious and wakeful world.

We live in profound times of opportunity. In reading the newspaper we can feel overwhelmed by the daily crises that seem to jump from the headlines. Yet, we know that crisis and chaos can be pivotal ingredients for insight and change – they often force choices we were previously blind to. Times like these beg us to listen and also to heed the messages we receive.

As you read this book, please consider it an invitation. The energies which have spoken through me may feel dormant for you, yet they bid you to dance with them. The rhythm and music may feel strange. You may resist the first steps. But if you relax into and absorb it at your own pace, you'll discover that not only is this dance liberating and wondrous – it will transform our world!

Llyn Roberts, M.A.

August 12, 2006

1

We are Stars

Remember that we can release
all that binds us in each moment
– we can manifest Light and transcend
through love in every moment.

Welcome. We are Light beings, Guardians of the Light. We, star beings, are spirits yet we are only separate from you in form. We are your higher, separated aspects that wish to rejoin you and celebrate in shared form.

We understand the transition to becoming Light and feel your changes – we are happy to meet consciously with you now. We come as workers of the Light at this needful time and must complete our destiny with regard to the earth. Our mission is clear and our hearts are open. Remember your true nature.

✳

The memory of our basic nature pulses yet cut off from our

hearts, we're still searching for wholeness. Only in being patient will we find the inner peace we seek. We are all able to heal the split we feel from spirit, yet first must see what's happening and surrender to the great momentum arising now.

The veils are falling. We're children of illusion, aware of only a small aspect of reality – yet we'll soon expand into our true form. There's so much more to know and experience. The mind has made us feel separate yet it's time for the rational mind to take its seat so our greater aspects can wake up.

The veils will slip away – what was hidden will be seen and brilliant Light will shine for us all. It's time for masters to awaken. Seekers, open your hearts, the call for change beckons. As the earth awakens we can rediscover who we really are, yet only when we're aligned can we gain the help to do so. Star beings can help us prepare, they provide the gateway for us to move through change more easily. Opening to our starry aspects helps us to reclaim who we are.

It's time to awaken to the delightful aspects of reality – we can wake up to a greater reality and experience our divine nature. The God Essence will consciously express through humankind.

Concerning this message, follow your intuition and pace your reading. Read this book when you feel alert, refreshed, and desire to do so, and stop reading when you get tired. This material doesn't only address your rational mind; the power of it lies beyond that.

Remember that we can release all that binds us in each moment – we can manifest Light and transcend through love in every moment.

Summon your highest intentions to direct the changes that come. Know that our starry sisters and brothers, and many others, are here to help us pass into Light and beauty. They assist our return to the universal life force.

2

The Sentient Earth

*As we synchronize with the earth as
one living, breathing, vibrating being
we will not destroy and neglect her.*

It's time to open and expand. When we know the true nature
of our world we will become one with it.

Change is here, this is a call to new times. Because the
times have ripened and enough of us are wishing it to be so,
the earth is becoming conscious. As it awakens, earthly beings will be blessed with an outpouring of energy that spawns
new life. As this energy releases into the universe, darkness
will become Light.

It's true that over time the earth, which is also sentient,
has become burdened by the ways of humankind. We're out
of balance and all of earthly life is impacted by our thoughts,
choices and actions. But understand that we choose each
moment and the past controls us only when we don't release

through the earth. This is the earth's gift to us. We are symbiotically tied and the earth can absorb and transmute energy. This is a pure and straightforward relationship – the more 'earth–bound' we become, the 'lighter' we become. As we synchronize with the earth as one living, breathing, vibrating being we will not destroy and neglect her. We will each open to our greater purpose. See how we and the earth are one – the more we poison and pollute her, the denser and more separate we become. Our egos are solidified.

To change, we must purify and only by aligning can we do this. We must dissolve what holds us back in order to lighten. As the momentum of the past is rekindled each moment, connecting with the earth burns karmic debris so each moment can be created freshly. Light then shines and nourishes us as we expand into universal energy. The earth wants to resonate with those who remember their own Light. Many of you have incarnated to help this shift – you are beacons of Light sparking remembrance in others.

Remember to be loving and expansive. The earth's consciousness, developing and pulsing at a higher rate, will help us to wake up. We'll realize many things we do not now. In aligning our power and energy with the earth we'll shine our Light, radiating endless energy to create. With joy, we will pass into Light.

To do so we must harmonize with the Mother, the life force in all things, she who gives life. We connect with the Mother through the earth. Light shines out to the world when we join in higher purpose – many are healing the earth and their sense of separation from her.

As we purify with the earth the Mother will nourish us. This begins with the root, the base of our physical system, the seat of our life force. The earth is an energetic system and we aren't separate from it – we're one with it. The earth's power is beyond words. Endless possibilities have been overlooked, veiled by our separation. The root of our physical system emanates power that many of us never experience. Opening at the root grounds and protects us as it's here that we and the earth are one. The energy of the root is like a volcano in that it's volatile yet earthbound, solid. It's fiery and red. Energy accumulates at the root and begins to move up. It's like a furnace in our body which must be kindled to ignite our *spiritual* fire. 'Riding the Earth' kindles this fire.

'Riding the Earth' allows the earth's energy up, into and through our root. This awakens our sexuality, moving energy up through the body. Our bodies are instruments of ecstasy. It's pleasurable to experience the body as one with the earth – this makes us feel open and awake. The best way to do this is to sit upon the earth.

Riding the Earth

Rousing the Inner Fire

1 Go to a quiet place in nature where you can sit for a while

undisturbed. Sit with your bottom directly on the ground. Take some time to look at everything around you – plants, trees, stones, soil, grasses, the sky, water, animals and insects. Also notice the smells, breezes, temperature and sounds of nature. *Feel* the life all around you. Now close your eyes.

2 Rest your mouth slightly open to relax your jaw and breathe simply all the way into your lower abdomen, focusing on the immediate experience of your breath, body and environment. Feel the sensations of air moving in and out of your nostrils and mouth, and feel the rhythm and movement of breath in your body. Allow yourself to relax.

3 As you breathe, also allow your buttocks and anus muscles to relax, keeping your root and sexual area open energetically. Rest your body sensually upon the earth and remain with these sensations as long as you wish, or until you feel full and complete.

4 Now imagine that you're breathing intense, volatile, and pleasurable energy up from the earth and into your root. You may see this energy with your inner vision yet you do not need to see it as *experiencing* it is the important thing.

5 Allow this energy to tingle and open the lower part of your body. Allow sexual feelings and pleasure to arise and let yourself fully experience this rousing. These sensations will still your mind and open you. Feel the pleasure as the earth pulsates into your root and let these sensations ripple through your entire body. Open to pure pleasure.

These sensations will ride up through your body. They'll begin with the root where you are physically one with the earth, and culminate at your crown. Stay with the experience until it naturally subsides.

6 Take time afterwards to stretch and relax, or take a leisurely walk.

As we are one with the earth we can enjoy each other intimately and we can't survive energetically without this relationship. Connect through your root. By making love with the earth you'll invite her energy and generosity. Don't feel embarrassed about this as sexuality sources life – life arises from the innate desire to be one with the cosmos, as well as the desire to be born from this union. The sexual energy links all life forms and keeps our bodies healthy. It's the physical seed of the soul's expression.

This path is profound and simple, yet we can only reconnect through exertion. For openness to happen we must 'will' personal and planetary change. The earth needs us. Tending her will clarify many things and heal our fundamental split. Ours and the earth's needs aren't separate.

All plants, animals and natural energies are affected by the actions of humankind. We've neglected to live harmoniously with other life forms, yet there are ways to change this. First, we must acknowledge this split. Stop and look squarely out to the world – see from your heart what's happened and realize that we've been blind. We think that we see, yet we do not see. We do not truly see our world for what it is, nor do we see the impact of our actions.

Life has become habitual. We're disconnected from the earth and from what sustains, purifies and energizes us. Everything is lovingly provided, yet our hearts starve from disconnection and our bodies numb from the reactive ways we live. There is a fundamental lack of rhythm. We've forgotten our intrinsic connection to nature and the stars, as well.

We must wake up and live from our deepest longings – we must conceive of how to shift our world. Listen closely to your inner voice.

3

Opening the Heart

There is a stirring in your soul.
This is the stirring of your highest
self, your highest potential.

The God Essence – however we define or experience God – is found within us all. At this level there is stillness, yet a vast dynamic energy. This energy moves toward universal wholeness, creating a momentum that longs to express through form. This results in the birthing, without exception, of every physical aspect of our world. From this point there is a further longing for the highest expression of Light within physical form. This Light awakens all form to its inherent 'God Essence', unifying energy that wishes to be experienced as love. Love, then, triggers the return to universal consciousness.

This is why the heart is so important. Universal love unfolds a new way of being. Love helps us push through illusion and opens us to blend with cosmic energy. Opening the heart quickens us and accelerates spiritual purpose.

The heart has many expressions. Its way is always simple and direct, yet untapped my many. Why is this so? We've closed our hearts through fear and fear makes us feel separate. Because we feel separate, we believe we need to protect ourselves. We do this by contracting our beings which restricts the flow of energy through our bodies. Without free–flowing energy and an open heart, we're divided. We become directed by a fearful mind which disconnects us from reality and the energy of the earth. The heart unites heaven and earth. It balances us so that we open to universal love. This love is unconditional, reverberating out to every manifestation of the God Essence.

Forgive yourself. Do not hold things within. It's not helpful to harbor negativity as this solidifies your world. We solidify through negativity and separation and create pain and preoccupation for ourselves. Let go of this preoccupation and take a moment now to rest into your breathing and feel your heart. Remember that when centered here, you are open and free.

Love transforms us on all levels and our heart must be open for us to lighten. We must also be one with the earth to ground and accelerate this process. We are one with the universe and must remember why we were born, we must remember our purpose. It's time to open.

Open to your heart's deepest expression. Have you heard and felt your deepest longings? Allow these to surface. You may see that they may not be reflected in the world around you, but don't let this stop you. Don't let fear overcome you as things won't change without these deepest yearnings surfacing. They will open your heart.

There is a stirring in your soul. This is the stirring of your highest self, your highest potential. It's important to open to this raw energy and let it ripple through every cell of your being. It can be a painful and deeply emotional opening yet you must let these feelings ripple through. Let your heart and body guide this flow and nurture through the process. Allow it to be until you feel at peace. When you come to a peaceful point you'll have a more open heart. Taste the nuances of this shift, savor them fully. Feel the quality of body, emotions and mind. Relax into this feeling and remember who you are.

'Riding the Earth' fills our body and being with the Light of our true nature. This way we can trust and stay connected to our deepest selves, knowing that all is well. We are well loved. Do not let confusion overcome you during these times.

Opening the Heart

Loving the Life Force Within

1 Find a comfortable place to sit where you won't be disturbed. Look around carefully, appreciating the details of your physical environment. Feel the sensations of the floor or earth beneath you and become aware of the space

below, around and above you. Orient yourself completely to your physical surroundings.

2 Next, stretch, easing any tension from your body. Rest your mind and let go of any preoccupations. Now close your eyes and be still. Focus on the rhythm of your breathing. Let it become softer and deeper as you relax.

3 Now, feel your heart. Feel the physical sensations first – feel the beat of your heart. Is there tension, constriction? Do you sense a color or temperature?

4 Now relax your mind. What do you *feel*? Do you feel sad, joyful, angry, loving? Allow your emotions to be as they are without trying to change them. Simply experience them.

5 Now allow your emotions to intensify. Experience them fully until you are flooded with feeling. Let these feelings rise in waves through your body, breathing deeply into them. Let them rise and ripple through your entire being, even rippling and riding beyond the boundaries of your physical body. Allow crying, howling, laughing, and writhing – whatever expression comes up. Let the energy, breath and emotions ride through every part of you and stay with your experience. Purely feel. Feel the power surging through you as you open your heart.

6 Now allow this energy to connect all the way down to your root and let your sexuality arise. Let yourself feel strongly and fully. Feel the powerhouse of energy and sense it travel upward as it intensifies. Let your whole body take delight in these feelings, breathing deeply with their movement.

Let the energy ride up through your whole body now and notice what you feel. You've integrated your system to a higher level; you have lightened your being.

7 Slowly come to a calm point, a still and peaceful place. Rest deeply within this space as your true home.

You are one with the universe and can realize this by opening your heart and body to experience higher levels of awareness. Your body knows the doorways to be opened – it's a pure vehicle of transformation.

Although you may feel troubled at times, put your troubles away to feel at peace. Indulge your heart to love yourself and others. Love is the door to openness. We begin with ourselves, with self-nurturance – tasting the sweetness of our beings opens us to the sweet taste of the world around us. Our hearts open and our spirits rise. We'll know wholeness and enter a natural flow that will bring Light to our entire beings.

Transformation is underway. Open your heart to the Light you are to bring heaven to earth.

4

Chaos, Time and Space

*We are continuous with the earth and
the stars – 'who we are' extends and
reverberates well beyond our bodies, in
fact pulsates widely beyond them.*

From an earthly perspective there are many ways to live; there
are many options and realities. This is an illusion. There's
only one way to live, and this is along the path of Light, ac-
cording to the laws of the universe. But how do we attain this
Light, how do we *become* It? Many become confused here and
this confusion can become an obstacle if we don't recognize
it. Because we don't see who we are, we desire to bring in the
Light that we already are. We are caught in duality.

The way toward Light involves the notion of 'chaos'. This
is complex, yet helps us understand how things are changing
now. Let's try something. Allow your mind to relax for a moment without preconception and say the word – Chaos. What
does this evoke for you? Feel these sensations in your body.

Now relax. Chaos must be integrated. It's the gateway to the future.

The call now to embody chaos tells us that things aren't always as they seem. Life just isn't what we think it is. How can we open to a larger, more complex world that's at the same time – *simpler* – than how we see things now? This is necessary and it's challenging. To do so, we must open our perception to include logic outside a linear view, relaxing habitual ways of interpreting and bringing things to conclusion. Fully entering chaos demands energy and an opening to our higher selves. It demands that we let go of 'who we *think* we are'.

Order and chaos are conceptual illusions. Being Light involves suspending what we believe so we can see things as they are in each moment. When the moment is experienced as it is, the illusions that hold us so firmly relax.

This is something we have to practice and our body is the best vehicle for this because it gets us out of our heads. As the way we think solidifies our world we must let go of this tendency to manifest fully. We have to stop manipulating and judging everything – we're asked to literally *feel* our way within these times as our rational minds will not carry us further. When we release the dominant hold of the mind, we're free.

More energy is available to us when we liberate ourselves, by liberating our ideas about the way things are. Anchor Light within your body, open to your higher purpose, and see how expansive you are. 'Letting go' will help this change, and relaxation is the key to letting go. Don't fear who you are. Relax the tendency to solidify. In becoming more relaxed you'll see that what you desire you create, and, what you believe you see. There's another approach that blends the relative view of reality with the absolute. This is how to shine the love and Light that you are.

Let's look at time and its relationship to our reality.

As we enter the time/space continuum we become contained, defined and limited. All of 'who we are' isn't reflected within the time/space continuum. But we can free ourselves with this truth and learn to see time differently. Time is fluid and concurrent to our thoughts. How we think creates the *illusion* of time as well as space. Cutting through the solidity of these perceptions opens us to a different way of seeing and being. This is something many of us know intellectually, but to change ourselves and our world we have to *experience* it. Conceptualizing creates, yet also limits who we are. The mind is not inherently a problem, but has forgotten that it's one with our body and one with the universe. When we open the doors of our conceptual mind we will see far more than we ever imagined. In this way we won't limit our experience.

Our experience of time is linked to how we see the world. Non–conceptual mind doesn't know time in this way. Within our reality things seem separate. Yet if we look deeply into the time/space continuum we see no such boundaries and the conditions that solidify the illusions of time and space now waiver. Time is a mirror, an illusion allowing a reflection of 'self'. This is how ego and separateness are maintained. Without time things would not seem so separate. But as our sense of time and ego also allows us to define and create our world, *obliterating* it isn't the answer – instead, we can simply move beyond its confinement. Seeing *through* the illusion of time allows us to be another way.

First, we must understand that not all of 'who we are' lives within this time and space, only a small aspect of us does. The individualized ego has a hard time seeing the greater view of who we are and our connection to all things. It's as if a part of us is compartmentalized, and we only know that part defined by time and space – we've forgotten the rest of who we are. The reflection crystallizes as ego, or individualized 'self'. But this is a solid and limited self. To know our true selves we must to look beyond the reflection. Look deeply within to know the expansiveness of your own being and remember that you must be fully in your body to do this.

By committing to our immediate physical experience, we transform. We come to an understanding that includes the time and space we now occupy but is not governed by it. When we're fully in our body and firmly on the earth our consciousness expands. To be one with the earth is to be at one with everything and to experience vastness – this is our true nature.

Recognize this in your daily life and moment to moment experience as the reality of this truth must seep deeply within. Many live exclusively from the mind and must soften this tendency to synchronize with greater reality. Ego maintains itself mainly through the intellect so the mind must learn to rest its hold. Here are some practices that will help:

Meditation

Resting the Mind

1 Seat yourself comfortably without distractions. Rest your mind. Take some deep breaths and do some gentle stretching. Staying with how your body feels right now, close your eyes and relax more deeply. Surrender to the world of the body to go within. This will become easier with practice.

2 When you feel connected and relaxed, notice the quality of your mind. Your thoughts fluctuate constantly – relax with this. There's no constant form to your mind. Have a sense of 'witnessing' the mind. Allow whatever to come up – thoughts, images or feelings – without either denying or getting wrapped up in them. Simply watch. Now again settle into your body. Feel the sensations of the breath moving in and out, focusing gently on the out–breath, yet letting it occur naturally. With each breath out now, feel that your thoughts flow out with them and dissolve into the space around you.

First, we must rest our minds. From the foundation of a restful mind we can become one with the greater energies

available to us from the earth and the heavens. These energies can be taken in and expanded throughout our bodies,
yet there is no way that the mind alone can do this. We
are continuous with the earth and the stars – 'who we are'
extends and reverberates well beyond our bodies, in fact
pulsates widely beyond them. We must experience this
to move beyond the relative mind that separates us from
greater reality. Remembering our connection to all things
revitalizes and replenishes us.

Wheels of Time

Expanding into Universal Time

1 Sit in a comfortable position, taking a few moments to
stretch and breathe deeply. Relax. Now close your eyes.

2 Imagine a rapidly spinning wheel of energy suspended in
the space just in front of you. This wheel spins so fast it
appears a blur. As you watch this wheel spin your body
feels heavy, solid and weighted. Tension may cloud your
mind and emotions. You realize that this spinning wheel
which exists *outside of you* is the 'Wheel of Linear Time'
– its motion seems to pull energy from you making you
feel tired and constricted.

3 Now take a deep, restful, cleansing breath as you completely release this visualization. Let go of any constriction
or heaviness in body, mind and emotions. Take another

deep breath and relax completely. Feel your body. Experience each breath fully, feeling the sensations in your body and the space around you.

4 Now feel that you're sitting comfortably at the *center* of *another* spinning vortex of energy. This is the 'Wheel of Universal Time'. The wheel is a luminous circle of Light spinning rapidly all around you. This wheel radiates Light through twelve energetic spokes into your luminous and physical bodies, nourishing, energizing and awakening you. Sit embodied at the center of this vortex – fully present in this time/space. Feel yourself at the same time, expanding beyond it. You will feel filled with Light. You are vast and free. Fully embody all dimensions and aspects of yourself in each present moment.

5 Feel the Light infusing you from the twelve spokes. Feel Light illumining your cells, organs, bones, muscles, tissues, mind and emotions. The Light pools to create a column of energy in the center of your body that moves up through you, connecting from your root deep into the earth and radiating out the top of your crown. Stay with this experience for awhile. Breathe into it – *feel*.

6 Now, let the visualization fade, yet staying with the feeling of this Light – allow its energy to integrate naturally. Transition slowly, remaining in an expanded, yet grounded state. Let this Light continue to infuse every part of your body, as well as your life, as you move through your day.

These practices help us enter each moment fully, expanding our sense of time and space. The way we might experience this is as if time has stopped, or become elongated. These times call for expansion on every level within each present moment. We must rest completely within every moment and expand that sense of rest to every breath, every movement, and every interaction that we make.

Embody these teachings. Allow them to seep within. Let fears and judgments arise and fall away naturally. When we rest within our true nature we're free – ego is dissolved, not into nothingness, but within the fullness of Light.

5

Energy Shifts and Transmissions

*The entire earth plane is shifting
– people, plants, animals, earth. Though
we may only glimpse this now, we are
one world and embody as one being.*

'Transmission' is an important part of the foundation of any energy change or progression. We can't rise to higher levels of vibration and reach expanded states of consciousness without them. Spiritual transmissions connect us to our higher selves – they enable us to experience and express more of who we really are.

The transmissions we're most familiar with are those given by someone, such as a spiritual teacher, who knows how to empower and awaken others. Ritual practices can also awaken us to higher levels of consciousness for specific purposes – such as Reiki attunements empowering hands–on healing.

In either case, our expanded consciousness then affects every aspect of us and our lives.

Another way we can receive transmissions is by initiating them for *ourselves*. We can deliberately attune ourselves to higher vibrations and expanded states of awareness. This can also happen spontaneously without our even realizing it – our higher aspects can wake up in any moment. Spontaneous transmissions are very natural, directed by our starry selves who assist our evolution through successive or simultaneous lifetimes. Energetic transmissions that open us to our higher purpose can also be provoked during illness, and 'difficult' or 'chaotic' times.

The third kind of energy transmission happens in nature, ignited by star or earth energies and involving spirit guides and helpers. Nature also teaches us, and transmits awakening energy to us, in our dreams. Directed by our higher selves we can be initiated to other levels of consciousness while we're sleeping.

Lastly, immediate and permanent shifts of consciousness can happen just by being in the presence of (sometimes even at great distances from), a highly attuned person. These shifts can happen quickly and unexpectedly but we won't experience them unless we're ready for them as we need to be pre–initiated in some way.

Transmissions deeply and permanently affect us and how we view the world. Each energy transmission has its own qualities, intelligence and movement, and we're all impacted uniquely. The initiation process awakens dormant energies in our subtle bodies which begin to resonate with accelerated frequencies. This ignites the path of our Divine Will so we can express more from our higher selves. These transmissions bring us closer to our true nature. Each initiation brings us closer to our spiritual purpose.

As transmissions open us to our greater purpose, the spirits who are connected to us may guide the process. Starry sisters and brothers, as well as other protector energies, also guide transmissions accelerating the earth's changes – the 'quickening' occurring now which is lightening the planet. We can't guide ourselves *through* this quickening unless we've let go enough of what holds us back, keeping us solid. Transmissions help us to remember our greater purpose as they help *lighten* us – although we can also fully wake up in any moment.

As heavy, karmic debris lifts, we gain new and vast perspectives on life reflecting higher vibrations. This can cause turmoil at times because as we integrate new perspectives, we must also release old habits and fixed ideas of who we are. 'How we see ourselves' and 'how we see the world' can shift dramatically. Follow your intuition to stay healthy and grounded through these changes. Connecting with your body and spending time in nature is essential – caring for the earth deepens our relationship with her which also grounds us. Moving your body in ways that inspire you will integrate energy changes into the physical. As you do this, feel and express the emotions that bubble up with your movement, to balance the flow of energy moving through you.

There are many shifts occurring on many levels. These are the stirrings of the heart and more deeply, the soul. The entire earth plane is shifting – people, plants, animals, earth. Though we may only glimpse this now, we are one world and embody as one being. The true nature of existence is within our grasp. Trust your process and guide yourself through this journey of Light with an open heart and an engaged will – know that you can overcome your obstacles.

When more balanced, we start to see the emanation of our own Light. As this happens we can glimpse a new way to be. Any changes we must go through to become balanced can happen with or without pain, upheaval, or other difficulties as we can choose to see through duality in any moment. The cleansing occurring on our planet and within us now, affects every part of us – karmic patterns and our orientation to time are relaxing. Time keeps us solid, but the momentum from deep within us now opens our hearts to Light.

As we open to our greater selves we naturally draw more Light. Opening to the energy pouring through us evokes an organic process where obstacles can rapidly arise. We may experience unexpected yet powerful emotions that quickly dissolve – we may release physical toxins and purge emotionally. Ride the wave of these changes and stay clear. Trust your process and you will accelerate the rhythm of cleansing and purifying. After clearing each obstacle, new levels of energy must be assimilated and integrated.

The best way to ground this energy into our bodies is to connect with the earth – bring the earth's power up, into and through your body for harmony and balance. Our power lies in our ability to integrate Light into the physical body and then to bring this Light into every part of our lives.

Constantly *opening* and constantly *grounding* is how to align. A natural rhythm develops here as energy heightens then integrates into the human system. We enter the flow of this rhythm by honoring our personal needs and desires, by indulging our hearts. Fully embracing life invites us to dance to a rhythm of opening and integrating, opening and integrating – in this way we will anchor and integrate as Light. Join thoroughly with your deepest aspects, *become one* with these, and obstacles will naturally fall away.

By harmonizing with the earth we begin to fall into rhythm together – by becoming one with the earth we speed up and smooth her process as well as our own. This union is comforting. The earth is naturally nurturing and healing, and she offers herself to us. Fully entering this relationship returns us to wholeness.

We are expansive beings of Light yet we have forgotten our true nature. Our minds are not enemies, but they must be reintegrated so we can be balanced and whole. It's time to release old ideas of self, other and world. Invite your beliefs to rise up so you can see them clearly and then it will be

easier to let them fall away. As this happens, there will be
nothing firm to orient to – just open space and Light. Do not
manipulate this space but simply rest your mind in it. When
the mind is empty humankind will move into a new way of
seeing which will make it easier to see the God Essence in
everything.

Let's open to the rhythm of these times and be free. We
don't need to 'act out' as deep shifts affect our entire psyche
and spirit from the inside–out. The path to transformation is
simple and direct – our hearts and bodies can guide us.

The illusion of being separate persists simply because of
how we've divided our consciousness. This must be resolved.
Remembering that *the Light body is not separate from the
physical body* helps us understand why we mustn't separate
from physical reality. The Light body comprises the physical
– the fabric of our body lightens to become the greater reality
– our bodies will transform. As form and matter are not solid,
your body will be you again as Light.

Embodying Light

Awakening Essence

1 Gently stretch your body then take several deep cleansing
   breaths. Let any tension gently ease with each out–breath.
   Feel the contact of the earth or floor beneath you and notice your posture. *Feel* your body. Now without trying to

change anything, notice the quality of your mind; is it fretful and preoccupied or as restful and spacious as a spring breeze? Simply notice.

2 Now, close your eyes and continue breathing at a normal pace. As you breathe, feel the air coming in and out through your nostrils or mouth and feel the movement of the breath in your body – undulating through your chest, abdomen, head, neck and spine. Feel the gentle inhalations and exhalations as well as the subtle contractions, expansions and rippling through your spine and torso. Keep breathing at a relaxed pace.

3 Now, in your minds' eye imagine a full length mirror directly in front of you. Look into this mirror and see yourself – you're completely made of Light. Light pulses through and radiates from your reflected mirror–body. As you look, you understand this is your true form. You are seeing your essence.

4 Keep looking in the mirror. Remember this Light as your true form. As you look, begin to breathe in and expel Light with every breath, radiating it in all directions. As you breathe in, your breath may deepen and intensify with the movement this Light brings. Keep breathing Light in and out. Let its frequency awaken you. *Feel* the pulsations. Continue breathing Light until your physical body becomes that Light–body in the mirror. Anchor the sensations of this into the physical.

5 Now gently let the visualization fade and return to a

normal pattern of breathing. Come to a point of rest, yet continue to feel the sensations of Light. Lie down to rest for awhile or go for a gentle walk and invite this awareness to integrate into your everyday life.

Synchronize by not separating 'spirit' from 'body'. Dissolve duality to experience oneness with the cosmos and to be at peace with yourself. Energy creates endlessly and as every form expresses Light, we must remember our *own* Light. In disassociating we cut ourselves off from all that is to come. Remember that truth and universal peace lie within – rest fully and become one with the universal life force.

6

Gathering

*We must join together to share our
spiritual gifts. Many of us have been
waiting for this time and it has come.*

All relationships trigger the return to universal awareness in
a way that can be consciously pursued. Opening to the raw
energy of our encounters makes it easier for us to see that
they aren't solid – relationships move and flow with the Light
that brings them into being. Acknowledging this flow helps
us understand that all things live to be as one with all other
living things. The magnetism that brings people together is
that same Energy that longs to see Itself as one Being.

All relationships have higher purpose and their means
may vary greatly. To be open and awake in our relationships we must see all others as aspects of the larger whole.
All situations arise from the desire to awaken fully and all
relationships provide what is needed to reclaim our alien-

ated aspects. Relationships should be seen as mirrors, and allowed to reflect those hidden aspects that are asking to be seen as 'us'. The teachings that come from such mirroring are often unexpected.

It also helps to nurture connections that encourage our full expression. Cultivate relationships with people who support your spiritual journey by embracing all aspects of your world. This way, when doubts arise, you'll move them more quickly. The snags that can hold us back are minimized when we have a spiritually supportive community that acknowledges and celebrates all of who we are.

Gathering is helpful. Join with others who desire love in their lives again. The hopefulness you feel together will remind you of the life you've forgotten – it will open you to ground as 'one' energy, in a way that can foster new perspectives and possibilities for experiencing the world. Being with others who are opening to the energies of the cosmos *quickens* us.

An 'assembly' is a gathering together of like–minded souls. Many are awakening to their true nature but are unsure of their experiences – fear of being rejected and isolated affects their ability to move forward. It's important to gather, to assemble, because assembling amplifies the experience of our own wholeness. It supports us in accepting and experiencing all of who we are.

Messengers of the Light may attract gatherings with those able to hear their expression of the truth yet there is no need to create 'followings'. Gatherings should be directed from the heart toward the highest good – and they should empower *everyone*. One of our biggest obstacles is our persistence in having someone *else* show us the way which makes liberation difficult. We must relax the tendency to project our own divinity onto others.

Gatherings are more helpful if the same group of people meets consistently. It's important to begin to resonate as 'one' and to let go of the need to be anything else but who we are. There's nothing to accomplish. The stillness of our hearts when gathered together and opened to each other radiates our wholeness. Meeting with an on–going group accelerates our ability to open to larger and universal energies that can expand consciousness – our joined energies open portals to higher awareness.

Many are ready to gather. Ground yourselves well. Become one with the earth and bring her energy up and into your bodies. Remember that as a group you are one body and one energy. Because the earth is a highly attuned being – by connecting and bringing her energy into your bodies, you will reach a higher resonance. **The earth radiates Light**. She has great gifts to bestow. By being one with her you will naturally ground and open.

For seekers, it's painful to forget our true nature, to experience separation from spirit and the earth. As illusion is maintained by ignorance many are still not conscious of this separation – it's usually those who seek who become aware of the truth earlier than others, which can make them feel isolated. Yet you are the forerunners of the coming times. You are beacons of Light to your communities and shouldn't despair.

The time has come for us to gather. We must join together to share our spiritual gifts – many of us have been waiting for this time and *it has come*. Our gifts are connected to these times of change and we carry great messages for humankind among us. We remember our own Light and are moving toward manifesting it.

It's important to recognize the special beings that come to help the planet at this time. Many of our children pave the way to our liberation – they dance within the Light and remember the true nature of their being. Many evolving now are very conscious and gifted with special attributes and abilities. They *remember* their true origin and are born to shine the Light for others. Great beings can amplify us and awaken our inner truth so we, too, may return. Through their contact we can rise to a higher state and adjust through many changes. We must listen to our hearts and allow their influence.

All of us must align with the Light of our higher purpose. Many fear their path because they fear themselves, which makes life habituated and difficult. Many are ripe to hear this call yet need help to do so. Open your hearts and minds to help those who have forgotten to remember but don't 'proselytize' or push 'beliefs' out to others. Focus your awareness

and hold in your thoughts those energies and messages connected to the highest good.

Luminous beings Light our path and honor our passage.
We can align within their circle of Light.

Circle of Light

The Luminous Core is Who You Are

It's preferable to do this practice as a group in a quiet place
although it can be done individually and when or wherever
desired.

1 Gather together and sit in a circle. Do some gentle stretching and take a few deep breaths. Hold hands now and take
  some time to look at each member of your group, feeling
  your connection with each person in the circle. Now close
  your eyes. Rest your mind and relax into your breath.
  Concentrate for a moment on the rhythm of your breathing,
  allowing it to come to a peaceful flow.

2 Stay with the sensation of your breathing, allowing each
  breath to awaken the memory and reality of Light. Open
  to your own Light, the Light of your soul. Consciously acknowledge that you are a luminous being and a transcend-
  ent soul of Light, reinforcing this feeling with each breath
  in and out. Again it's important to *feel* this Light infusing
  you, more than worrying about seeing it.

3 Now allow yourself to feel the luminous and sparkling

quality of your own Light being breathed in and out through every pore. You may find that you see this as well, but make sure you stay with the feeling of it in your body. Feel that you're at one with all else that radiates as pure Light.

Remembering Light will quicken you to the circle of Light. You may feel as if Light beings are *de*-scending into a circle around you or that you are *a*-scending into a circle of Light beings.

4 When you clearly feel the strength of your own Light and are one within the circle of Light beings, open your heart to a deep sense of peace. Breathe this peace deeply into yourself and then out to the circle again, immersing in the feeling of being one with this Light. Let any emotions that are bubbling up move through to cleanse and comfort you.

Feel yourself within this circle, blessed by the power of your luminosity. You emanate Light, naturally pouring it out to all that's around you. To always know this connection, open to your luminous core.

5 When you feel ready, open your eyes and do some gentle stretching, coming fully back into the room. Go around the circle and connect with each person in whatever way you're drawn.

Your yearnings for Light, love and unity are real. Surrender to your path and you'll receive and flow freely. Fine tune yourself to the frequency of Light beings and rest within the Light. We are one with these beings in Light and love and they are ever by our side. Feel the brilliance of the Light that is us all replenishing you – this will open you to see that we are one.

7

Re-Earthing

You are the earth, the stars, and the moon. You are one endless piece of the universe that is us all and with which we must reconnect.

Light is our home and it's our sustenance. Coming back to the Light will guide the earth and its healing. We carry within us everything needed to be luminous beings living harmoniously with our planet.

Begin to see the earth as a being that is pulsating, sentient and awake. Trust her intelligence and intention. Fully integrate yourself with her energy. We must acknowledge that the earth is our mother and cultivate and honor our relationship with her. Because we are one with the earth we may sometimes experience accelerated shifts of consciousness during the changes that are occurring now. We must open to our inner wisdom and synchronize with her so we reverberate as one. We can access this wisdom individually, but connect-

ing with the earth in groups will accelerate the journey and
purify us.

We and the earth are made of sacred elements which com-
prise all of earthly life – it's time to embrace the elements
and open to the primordial energy of physical form. The earth
is a generous, compassionate being who offers herself to us,
but to experience this generosity we must re-establish our
inherent connection. Reverberating as one opens us to the
earth's nurturance and sustenance.

The five sacred elements are earth, air, water, fire and
spirit. Our bodies require these energies and they help us experience our intrinsic wholeness. As it's only an illusion that
we're separate, reconnecting makes us whole again – as we
and the earth are one, there's love and remembrance awaiting
us that we have little awareness of now. Human beings are
open conduits of energy that can link the earth and the stars.
We hold great potential. As conduits of energy we can bring
to the earth, wisdom, power and energy from other dimensions. But to channel and stabilize these cosmic forces we
must first be one with the earth – and fully in our bodies.

We've begun to experience our oneness with the earth
through the practice of 'Riding the Earth'. Realize that we
don't just purify *with* fire in this practice, we *become* fire – this
idea strikes intuitively for many because of the deeply buried
energies that wake up when the spiritual fire is ignited. Fire
that arises from the root through 'Riding the Earth' is shared
by the earth and becomes one with the energy of our bodies.

When we become *one* with the element of fire we become purified and experience the possibility of life with ecstasy.

So, our healing begins with the earth and the five elements. In our own bodies and in the earth's body, fire is the purifier that opens the path for spirit; water brings fluidity and balances the flow of spirit; air is the conduit, the medium through which spirit is channeled; and the element of earth grounds the entire process so the physical forms of the earth – and our bodies – can hold the energy. This is a simple view of how spirit flows through the earth and human bodies. Earth, air, water and fire offer themselves as conductors for this process. But on an absolute level none of the elements are separate and the fifth element, spirit, permeates them continuously – communicating between, and infusing all life forms. The fifth element, spirit, opens us to the cosmos. Spirit flows freely for those who open. Openness arises from intention. It is born from the seed of our Divine Will which fuels our higher purpose.

As we are one with the elements, spending time in nature invites the sun, trees, rivers, winds, stones and sky to feed and replenish us. The earth can renew us – and we must also give back to her what we can. Communicate with the life all around you, connecting with plants, animals, and natural energies that want us to see them as they are. They are extremely sensitive to the changes happening now and are open to us. We must align with these children of the earth and see that her beauty manifests through them. Hearing their voices, we'll become one with our world. They'll open our heart and purify us.

Slow down to connect with nature. We're moving so quickly that experience is blurred and muted and we're not truly living in our physical bodies. If we were synchronized and living fully in our bodies we would be naturally vibrant beings of Light. Slowing down is the key. Slow down activity, distraction, discursive thought – invite quiet and stillness as a friend. We aren't losing or wasting time, but opening our hearts to universal love. We must feel peaceful and restful ourselves to extend true compassion to the world. When peace and stillness dominate our own hearts we rest in our true form. In this way our actions arise from, and generate – *unity* – instead of disconnection.

Our senses awaken from this point of rest. In taking the time to respond to the beckoning of the world around us we'll receive energy and awaken. The earth is always calling us to remember that we and she are one. But we have to hear and respond so we can receive the gifts of the natural world. The world is a place where Light and energy are abundant, shifting and flowing – all things give and receive in this way and are intrinsically one. We have cut ourselves off from this loving flow of life and are being depleted because of this separation. Invite your senses to the world around you. Begin with the *natural* world – the earth herself – as we must heal this division before all else.

Immersing in nature helps us see each form of life as a

precious gift of spirit. When this happens we'll shift away from duality.

Gazing

Opening to Natural Energies

You are a star gazer. Gazing is your gateway home. Gazing will help you return to your true self. You are the earth, the stars, and the moon. You are one endless piece of the universe that is us all and with which we must reconnect. You must bring gazing once more into your life. This practice will connect you to a childlike energy that is free and pure and expansive. It will open your heart to the larger energies around you. The best place to gaze is in nature.

1 Go to a peaceful place in nature where you won't be disturbed. Sit down and close your eyes. Let your body be in firm contact with the earth and feel the energy of the earth seep into you gently but powerfully. Feel your oneness with this sweet flow. Feel the heaviness of your body and the solid earth beneath you. Make this a visceral experience, really *feel* it. Peace is the gift that a solid sense of resting on the earth can bring. Relax into this relationship, knowing you are at home upon the earth. Rest this way for awhile, relaxing further with each breath. Breathe fully, as if you are breathing into the earth as well.

2 When you feel ready, open your eyes and look out. You

will quickly find what you wish to gaze upon. It may be a slowly moving stream, a tree, some stones, a patch of grass, a blue sky or starry night. Let yourself be drawn intuitively and gaze softly upon what draws you. Taste and feel its qualities, imagining that you are actually touching its energy and sensing its subtleties. Savor these feelings. They may spark curiosity, or a wish to enter more fully into that which you see. Let this feeling rise. You are opening in appreciation. Your mind is resting. You are looking not only with your eyes but with your whole body and your whole energy being. You will enter a timeless space.

3 At some point you may experience an energetic shift, a change in what you're feeling. You might feel like you are 'popping through' into a space that is dynamic, moving – you will feel that you're one with what you look at. In a sense, you will no longer be looking. You will *be* that which you gaze upon. When this happens, *feel* your body and the earth beneath you. You'll be moving energetically within a larger space than your body. You're mixing dimensionally and opening beyond the boundaries of your physical body. Take your time. Relax into this shift. You may feel strong emotion and your body may feel expansive. You're touching the energy of the universe. The movement of this energy and the pulsation it brings to your body may surprise you. Stay with your experience for a few moments.

4 The energy will naturally begin to dissipate and as it does, take your time until you feel peaceful. Then close your

eyes and rest. You can lie down if you want and you may sleep deeply. Your body has been energized to a new level and must rest to assimilate and integrate the energies. Allow yourself to simply be at peace. Rest deeply into your being, sleeping undisturbed. When you wake up you will feel loving, tender and refreshed.

This practice will ground and quicken you. It re-awakens you to the natural energy of the world.

8

Synchronicity and Will

*The union we experience when
synchronized in mind, body and
spirit dissolves the illusion that
separates us from universal energy.*

This is the time to be awake and aware. It's the time we've
been waiting for and we're innately capable of meeting it.
Trust that spirit flows through all things and join your higher
purpose with your awareness – you will awaken to see the
Light in everything.

A shift in consciousness helps us remember that we are
great beings of Light. This initiates a birthing process with
its own pain and passage, yet like our physical birth, we'll
emerge into an expanded world. Warm and loving beings will
welcome us as we awaken.

Our Divine Will propels this awakening. The world can
become solid and reactionary when the will, the higher self,
lies dormant and silent. When the Divine Will awakens,

spirit arises with strength and integrity. This ignites our Light body from the root up, mixing with the energy of the earth as it lightens. Our true nature becomes all pervasive, ultimately familiar, and has its own momentum.

We will *be* Light. We will experience who we really are, which we've never really 'come from', nor are we really 'moving toward' it. This is beyond linear thought. The result of this expansion is brilliance and compassion that radiates to everything and everyone around us. We *become* whole – *again.*

Self as a Puzzle

Re-membering Who You Are

1 Picture yourself as a puzzle. See your pieces strewn on the floor. You can almost see who you are yet you're not pieced together. The picture of you is not yet clear.

2 Now, move the pieces of 'you' around freely. Your sense of self will seem distorted and disintegrated. You are fragmented, yet all of 'you' is there – it's just not put together right.

3 Hold this image for a moment and notice what feelings arise with it. Take a moment to feel this fragmentation in your body. How does this feel? Very likely, you'll want to pull yourself together.

4 Now imagine that you're seeing yourself as a whole being and not fragmented at all. Imagine that this is who you have always been. See yourself for who you are now. Take the time to feel this wholeness in the core of your being.

See that you have the ability to heal yourself, to make yourself whole again. You are *already* whole, yet at the same time *returning* to wholeness. This is the universal momentum. Our will naturally strives toward wholeness because fragmentation is intolerable on a deep level. If your world disturbs you, see this as a reflection of the fragmentation you must come to terms with, and see that the world can change. Our higher will fuels the power for this change.

Remembering is the key and without it we can't move forward. Remembrance doesn't refer to a specific memory or lifetime but to the soul, our fundamental point of reference which evokes deep emotion. Synchronicity guides us on this journey and must be made conscious as great energy and remembrance are available at these times. As the longing in our hearts comes to fruition life pulsates and aligns, beginning to see itself as Light – the world mirrors our awakening through synchronistic events. Its dance is of union that reverberates out and draws back manifestation. Synchronistic events can also be messages to us from Light beings. As the veils between the worlds thin, we're able to glimpse an expanded reality.

Open your heart to realize your potential. As we attune to the flow of life we see that it has its own momentum. Our life force is a river of energy that lives and flows in consonance with the universal life force. When we flow consciously with this current we're limitless – we speed along with tremendous energy and resources. This is universal law. There are no more sporadic peak 'openings' of consciousness here and there because when we're synchronized in body, mind and spirit we're *always one* with universal energy. Knowing we're part of the larger whole helps us realize our greater potential. We understand we can't try to *be* that which we already *are*.

As we begin to expand, many shifts can occur that affect the mind. Remember to ground through the earth and in your body when you feel afraid and confused. Stay relaxed and open. Take the time to feel what you're feeling and let your feelings come up strongly, whatever they may be. By feeling the 'energy' of our fear it can move through our bodies – our emotions can wake us up. We can move fear to new levels of integration and open to the parts of ourselves we alienate the most. Your heart will open and flood with life-affirming energy as you reclaim your lost aspects. You'll be free to express your soul's purpose.

Waking up and expressing from the soul is about being who we are. This means that we should always be aware of the tendency to disconnect from our wholeness, because we can't transcend by splitting reality. *All* experiences show the way to the Light. By entering each experience fully we're one with the Light that arises. From this point of view obstacles are illusory – contradictions and the 'darker' sides of life are illusions as well. *Everything* in our world arises from and shares one source, Light.

When confused, experience your confusion. Be yourself during the most difficult and challenging times. Enter these as your own bloodstream, as if they weren't separate from you. Invite yourself to the feast of your own chaos and see it's here that you'll awaken. We can fully wake up in our darkest hour to experience a clarity and stillness that will open our hearts. Let go of what you hold. Become one with all you fear and let there be Lightness again in your being.

Don't 'believe' in anything too solidly. Don't make a plan out of this message and don't build a world out of it. Simply open to the depths of what *you* know as truth; this will bring wholeness. Align your being with your inner truth and let go of dogma to see that whatever arises is the play of Light.

Don't stop your life or what you're doing and don't abandon your world. Bringing Light to everything we do is what connects us with each aspect of our soul's emanation. Remembering experiences that have opened you to truth can help you to bring these into your day–to–day world – bring them into your life and infuse every detail of your ordinary life with your luminosity. Each of us can will ourselves to wake up and manifest in the moment. Our Divine Will helps us rise to a higher vibration that's always available.

The Mandala of Life

Igniting Wholeness

1 Imagine or *sense* a beautiful and intricate mandala spread before you. Its colors vividly depict the patterns and design of an elaborate silk border. There are also numerous

gateways to inner spaces in the mandala which lead to a defined center point. Visualize or *sense* your mandala in as much detail as you can.

2 Now take some time to feel which exact place in the mandala calls to you. No location is better than any other and the border is equally important as the center. What's important is that you find the place that is without a doubt, yours to claim.

3 Imagine now that you can enter this mandala from any direction or gateway to go to the location on the sacred form that beckons you. Notice how you enter and to where you're drawn.

4 When you find your place, *feel* yourself fully inhabit it. What does it feel like in your body to be here? In your heart? Claim your place in the mandala and summon all of who you are here without judgment or priority. *All* of who you are belongs here. This place is yours – it embraces and celebrates all your aspects without exception.

5 Harmonize within your place in the mandala, anchoring the full breadth of you here. Be fully present. Know that doing so calls all aspects and dimensions of you so the living energies of your place can awaken. Feel the Light that radiates from and all around you as you do this.

6 Now look out to the rest of the mandala. See its beauty. Notice others claiming their proper place within the whole. See them fully embrace who they are. See their Light begin to shine, and witness them awakening the living energies

of *their* spot on the mandala. Now see many parts of the mandala beginning to Light, illumining an ever larger area.

As you move through ordinary life, stay rooted in *your* place in the Mandala of Life. Shine your Light brightly – wherever and whoever you are. Awaken the living energies that wish to express through you.

Open your heart to the voice of your soul. Connect with the deep longings that appear day to day and moment to moment – yet which you may ignore and suppress. Cut through habituation to become one with the soul's voice in each present moment. This is the journey to who you are. Experience each moment, pursue it to its completion, and then release it. Awaken to your world and as you expand you'll see that limitations are illusions.

As more of us do this we'll draw together and ignite each other. We'll expand our Light to illumine the darker areas of consciousness to release obstacles. Division, confusion, and darkness are fuel for awakening from the illusion of separateness. Don't suppress your emotions but see that every aspect of your being is an expression of Light. From this point of wholeness we won't project our divinity *or* darkness so strongly, so our world may not appear as dualistic. Remember that your will propels this journey and your heart guides it.

To realize wholeness we must cut the illusory veils particular to our own karma. Only *we* can cut through to our larger and more expansive aspects. Take responsibility to know wholeness in each moment, regardless of what you think or feel – walking this path will empower you.

9

Light Manifesting

*We are coming to a time in our history
that will be like no other. The path we
walk will dissolve reality as we know it.*

Our goal is to fully experience and express who we are and
to do this we must open our minds to other ways of knowing
and being. Don't fear the universe opening to you in this way.
Relax into your fear and you'll easily find your way through
these times. There's abundant help available now, a living
stream of energy that we can connect with. We've never been
alone – we've always been many expanded energies and we
can now bring these into one form. Open and relax as you
know the way within your core. You've never lost this and
your heart will show you the way. You are free to lift the veils.
The Light you seek is the Light that is you.

We are coming to see our own Light. This Light emanates
from an inexhaustible source and flows through all living

things – our Light shines forth from our essence and interacts with every other aspect of life.

Life is a dance of frequencies that continuously intermingle, react to and affect one another. Everything engages in this dance. You are *not* a separate entity, identity, ego or physical organism. All is a web of Light and we are all interconnected – we all pulsate to a rhythm connected to this web which gives sustenance and life force to all forms. There is no life that's not connected to this Light.

It's important to connect with this web of Light and to see that it is we – as we are. This quickens us and we need only let go enough to consciously connect. It's quite simple though we may not find it so because letting go can bring fear. Let your fears arise but not control you – we must acknowledge our fears but then release them to be whole.

Surrender to the momentum that arises. Go further than ever before with your full truth. Let the veils fall. Fulfill your natural destiny and rise with others to the awakening of spirit within form. All who see the Light in themselves must move toward seeing the Light in all things. We must follow our individual direction to this destiny – this is how we will find that we are one.

We are all the web of Light, love and life. Star beings – are *us*. They are truly one with our being. We've simply cut our awareness off from the larger whole and experience difficulty seeing ourselves as that whole. We've forgotten our true nature, our true form, and our intrinsic connection to the universe. We must put the pieces back together to realize they've never lost their wholeness – we are vast and whole already. The challenge is to see this.

We must remember our expansive nature – the way to do this is to live life fully and become one with every aspect and detail of our world. We must *become* the fabric of our lives. We transcend by becoming one with every aspect of who we are. When we become one with the fullness, the density and the contradictions of our world, we see our own wholeness. All is seen for what it is and we transcend through fullness – our Light shines when we embrace all aspects of who we are.

Beams of Light are available to us now that weren't before – these are star energies from high sources, some from remote parts of the universe. These beams of Light are the essence of love, wishing our hearts to wakefulness. When we relax as we are, our hearts will open and anchor the memory of Light within us. These columns of energy are available to all beginning to see they are Light.

Beams of Light

Awakening Universal Love

1 Sit quietly and close your eyes. Relax your mind and body thoroughly. Harmonize with the rhythm of your breathing and the sweet essence of your life force. You are truly one with spirit and your body is a pure expression of this. Feel

this spirit fully united with your body and see yourself emanate Light.

2 Become aware of your breathing – *feel* the breath as you take pure, white and sparkling Light in through all your pores. Your entire being begins to breathe Light in and out and may pulsate forcefully with the frequency of this Light. You may have physical sensations of this Light blasting through you.

3 When you feel this, also notice your emotions. Focus in on the area of your heart. Keep breathing lightly and allow your breath to move with the pulsation of Light and emotion, until a rhythm begins here. Feel your heart open, strong and resonant with the energies that course through you. You are now ready to connect with an ever larger, purifying energy source.

4 Begin to imagine or sense a column, or a beam of Light that emanates from somewhere above the top of your head. Feel the power and the purity of this energy and its loving intention. At some point your crown will open and this pure beam of Light will pour into you at full strength. You will *be* this column of Light. As this happens, your consciousness releases then expands. You'll feel oneness with everything. As the Light pours through your heart, allow yourself to feel a warm, glowing love expand to all parts of you. Know this beam of Light as the path to oneness.

Oneness is experienced as love. Embody this beam, become

one with this Light to become whole. This is your destiny and your true form. This Light will literally pour forth from you and you'll radiate it out to others.

Remember your inherent potential. As Beings of Light you are called to illumine from the centerless center.

✳

We must embrace a relative reality, yet remember that any point of view is illusory. If we follow and believe in something, we must also release these beliefs. Absolute truth is related to openness and expansion – the full expression and acknowledgment of the truth in any given moment is what reveals its inherent Light. Every moment contains wholeness.

Each of us must avoid seeking truth outside ourselves which hinders the free and spacious flow of universal energy. The only way to transcend limitation is to see beyond it. We can follow no–one but ourselves to our genuine expression – we are our own liberators and there are no shortcuts. Many messages penetrate our reality. We must listen well and follow our hearts. Remember that in choosing consciously an internal process will synchronize and guide you. There is no other way to find truth except within and you should discriminate well. The only way to *remember* who you are is to *be* who you are.

As we will ourselves to see the Light in everything we'll awaken the inherent goodness that waits to be roused. We will see ourselves as the greater whole. Our divine journey on earth at this time will wake up what's separate and unique in each of us, bringing the God Essence into form. The God Essence is willing to see Itself through us, as we are.

Many life forms and worlds live beyond our own and all are trying to see themselves as Light in any way they can. Because the God Essence wants to see Itself in *all* things, all will be illumined. All will move to the expression of Light that knows Itself as God.

You are being called back to the Light. Do you realize this is the voice of your own soul? Do you realize that freedom begins with the desire to be free? No lines are drawn within our world that we do not draw ourselves. The illusion of separateness is painful but it will be released. We can release from the illusion to see the world as it truly is. Let Light fill you and remember the voice of your soul. When there's yearning for the soul's expression there is a longing to be filled with Light and to remember the voice of the God Essence as our own.

We are all moving toward wholeness. Wholeness is seeing things as they are and finding our rightful place within this order. Wholeness is always available to us. We are *already* whole.

Energy pours out now, energy which ignites the remembrance of Light. This energy awakens our more expansive aspects, beckoning them forward. As this energy moves through us, we will see ourselves as Light which will awaken the desire to see the Light in all things.

The natural evolution for humankind is to become fully conscious. Emanate love from your core and dissolve the solidity of your world. You will transform – spirit and matter will fuse. You'll be filled with Light and resonate higher and lighter than before. Reclaim the grace in your life. Open to grace and you will live it.

This time in our history will be like no other. The path we walk will dissolve reality as we know it. This is a time of purification and we know in our hearts this has begun. Changes will come. Prepare well and don't act out of fear and rebellion. Things are as they are and there's nothing to fight. We've deluded ourselves about the true nature of our world and the illusion is fading. We can use our fear to wake ourselves up.

Many accelerated energies impact the earth at this time which will continue to accelerate. You may find these vibrations difficult to accommodate. Bring in the Light – awaken and you'll be guided. Consciously choosing Light penetrates the denser layers of consciousness. Clarify your intentions and in recognizing that thought creates reality – shift your thoughts toward wholeness. As the mind expands there's greater compassion because we become synchronized with our higher aspects, including the earth, and radiate wholeness.

Many believe that we and the earth will experience great catastrophe during these times of change. Remember to be flexible concerning how change can occur and what it'll look like, so you don't miss the larger view. It won't help to prepare for change with fear–filled measures. Know that the earth wants only that we awaken – it is we who will choose how this happens. Our awakening must express wholeness.

These are times that stretch the soul. Remember the calling of your worldly purpose and follow that voice to where it naturally leads. We will find what we desire only in this way.

Becoming whole is the way to remember that we are stars. When this is realized we'll evolve and desire to manifest even more fully – we'll want to awaken our Light even more to express universal energy. In this way, the God Essence will remember that we are one. The God Essence will create another universe that consciously expresses body, mind and spirit.

10

The Good Remembering

*Choose to experience Light in every
situation whether you perceive it as 'good'
or 'bad'. When you do this, there is no
need to cling to or reject anything.*

The universe expresses itself in dualities; in a dance of light
and dark, of becoming and returning and of form and form-
lessness. As form evolves a natural momentum arises for the
God Essence to become conscious and to experience Itself.
This is primordial longing to return to the Star and eventually
dissolves the illusion of separateness.

The star that we are is beyond dimensionality and duality. It's the star that all things originate from and that all
return to. As we open to our heart's calling, a new force,
Light, moves through us and opens our starry centers. This
brings the remembrance of wholeness and Light and ignites
an inner flame that burns to move as one with the universal
life force.

In response to the great need in the world now, a new way is rising in the hearts of many. Many are beginning to see themselves as Lights in the world, illuminating the way for others. The way to shine *your* Light is follow your heart and be fully who you are. Understand that all things are Light and recognize all things as intrinsically good. This enables you to embrace any person and any situation. It creates an open–hearted center of love that beckons the lost back home.

The Good Remembering shows us that we have nothing to lose but our illusions about the way things are. Along the journey you may feel as if you're dying, you'll have nothing to hang onto. Choose to stay with your experience, seeing it not as the death of the self you've come to know, but the birth of your new life as Light. Keep this new life anchored in the heart. Your loving heart opens you to continual internal guidance that arises every moment. You can then be playful and trust each moment to reveal what's needed.

We are one star, we are one essence. Always remember this. As each individual awakens, more Light shines for us all to see who we really are. Arise to this new time in our world when all may awaken in their own natural and unique ways. Let this world remember that it can wake itself up. Remember your true nature and move in a way that makes illumination possible for all beings. This gives the God in us expression. All things must return to their essence to remember they are intrinsically one.

The Good Remembering tells us that because we are one being, it's necessary to care for our planet more than ever before. As we see ourselves for who we are we realize we can relieve suffering by taking a different approach to living. The confused state of our world can be unraveled in an environment of care and acceptance. All beings long to know themselves as God and to see that God is alive in every situation. Time, love and understanding are needed for all to discover their inherent God Essence. When this discovery is made the world will move as one being. The confusion that pervades the world now will be dissolved.

Remember, the universal movement is toward wholeness. Every moment and every action calls upon the heart to find its own way, to become one with the hoop of life and to return to source. Learn to dance with your own longing with child-like surrender. Have a hearty sense of humor! Remember the goodness of life and the joy that it can bring. Choose to experience Light in every situation whether you perceive it as 'good' or 'bad'. When you do this there is no need to cling to or reject anything. The natural luminosity of the moment is all that remains.

When all things remember their natural luminosity they rest in dynamic movement. They move through the world open heartedly, appreciating that separation creates the longing that moves them back to source. In this way the dance of life kindles a spirit that lives in all beings and moves as pure ecstasy.

About the Author

Llyn Roberts was born and raised in a French–Canadian Catholic community in south-eastern New Hampshire, in the US. *The Good Remembering* emerged from a profound spiritual awakening following the birth of her second child.

Llyn holds a masters degree in Tibetan Buddhist and Western Psychology from Naropa University and was a student of the late Chogyam Trungpa, Rinpoche. She has worked alongside indigenous shamanic peoples in remote parts of the world and runs the non– profit Dream Change, founded by author and environmentalist John Perkins. Roberts has been initiated into Quechua and Siberian shamanic circles, teaches in Europe and in the US at the Omega Institute and other learning centers. She lives in western Massachusetts. Llyn also co–authored (with Robert Levy) *Shamanic Reiki* (O Books).

For more information about Llyn Roberts and her work, and to learn about Dream Change:

www.thegoodremembering.com and www.dreamchange.org

Through the ages, spiritual teachers, healers and shamans have pointed us toward a world beyond this one; a world of powerful, loving energies, and beings of light. Their voices speak to us, and if we are prepared to listen, they will change our lives and the future of our planet. This inspired rendering of the collective wisdom of these voices draws on native traditions from around the world, offering a message from our ancestors of high caliber inspiration, a beacon lighting the path through changing times.

Prepare to lift the veils of illusion as you turn these pages, and as you do, you will learn that you play an essential role in the unfolding of the universe.

Brian Luke Seaward, Ph.D., founder of Inspirations Unlimited and The Paramount Wellness Institute.

A magical, powerful little book that transcends words and speaks directly to soul.

Melody Beattie, New York Times best selling author of *Co-Dependent No More.*

Everyone should read this book! Anyone interested in more fully participating in life will value it immensely.

Donald M. Epstein, D.C., Developer of Network Chiropractic.

Llyn Roberts shares in a brilliant way a new vision for the future. The Good Remembering *provides inspiration that we all need right now.*

Sandra Ingerman, author of *Soul Retrieval.*

LLYN ROBERTS works with John Perkins in Dream Change, applying indigenous wisdom for personal and global change.

ISBN 978-1-846940-38-5

9 781846 940385

BOOKS

Inspiration/New Age
£7.99
$16.95
www.o-books.net

Cover design by Design Deluxe Ltd.